# waking up
# from the
# dream of
# a lifetime

REALLIFESTUFFFOR**WOMEN** ON DISAPPOINTMENT

A NavStudy Featuring *The* **MESSAGE**®

Written and compiled by Karen Lee-Thorp

# NAVPRESS®

BRINGING TRUTH TO LIFE

## OUR GUARANTEE TO YOU

We believe so strongly in the message of our books that we are making this quality guarantee to you. If for any reason you are disappointed with the content of this book, return the title page to us with your name and address and we will refund to you the list price of the book. To help us serve you better, please briefly describe why you were disappointed. Mail your refund request to: NavPress, P.O. Box 35002, Colorado Springs, CO 80935.

The Navigators is an international Christian organization. Our mission is to reach, disciple, and equip people to know Christ and to make Him known through successive generations. We envision multitudes of diverse people in the United States and every other nation who have a passionate love for Christ, live a lifestyle of sharing Christ's love, and multiply spiritual laborers among those without Christ.

NavPress is the publishing ministry of The Navigators. NavPress publications help believers learn biblical truth and apply what they learn to their lives and ministries. Our mission is to stimulate spiritual formation among our readers.

ISBN 1-57683-862-5

Cover design by studiogearbox.com
Cover illustration by Jupiter Images
Creative Team: Steve Parolini, Arvid Wallen, Cara Iverson, Pat Reinheimer

Written and compiled by Karen Lee-Thorp

Some of the anecdotal illustrations in this book are true to life and are included with the permission of the persons involved. All other illustrations are composites of real situations, and any resemblance to people living or dead is coincidental.

Unless otherwise identified, all Scripture quotations in this publication are taken from *THE MESSAGE* (MSG). Copyright © 1993, 1994, 1995, 1996, 2000, 2001, 2002. Used by permission of NavPress Publishing Group. Other versions used include: the *Holy Bible, New Living Translation* (NLT), copyright © 1996. Used by permission of Tyndale House Publishers, Inc., Wheaton, Illinois 60189. All rights reserved.

Printed in the United States of America

1 2 3 4 5 6 7 8 9 10 / 09 08 07 06 05

FOR A FREE CATALOG OF NAVPRESS BOOKS & BIBLE STUDIES,
CALL 1-800-366-7788 (USA) OR 1-800-839-4769 (CANADA)

# contents

# about the
# REALLIFESTUFFFORWOMEN
## series

Let your love dictate how you deal with me;
    teach me from your textbook on life.
I'm your servant—help me understand what that means,
    the inner meaning of your instructions. . . .
Break open your words, let the light shine out,
    let ordinary people see the meaning.

—PSALM 119:124-125,130

We're all yearning for understanding—for truth, wisdom, and hope. Whether we suffer in the simmering quiet of uncertainty or the megaphone cacophony of disbelief, we long for a better life—a more meaningful existence. We want to be Women Who Matter. But the fog of "real life stuff" we encounter every day obscures the life we crave, so we go on with the way things are.

Sometimes we pretend we don't care.

*We do.*

Sometimes we pretend everything is fine.

*It isn't.*

The truth is, the real life stuff matters. In that fog, there are things about our husbands, our children, our friends, our work, and, most significantly, ourselves that cause varying degrees of distress, discomfort, and disease.

The REAL LIFE STUFF FOR WOMEN series is a safe place for exploring the truth about that fog. But it's not a typical Bible study. You won't find any fill-in-the-blank questions in these pages. Nor will you find any pat answers. It's likely you'll come away with more questions rather than fewer. But through personal reflection and—in a small group—lively discussion (the best part of a Bible study anyway), these books will take you where you need to go and bring greater hope and meaning to your life.

Each of the books in this series provides a place to ask the hard questions of yourself and others, a place to find comfort in the chaos, a place to enlarge understanding, and—with the guidance of the Holy Spirit—a place to discover Real Life Hope that brings meaning to the everyday.

# introduction

Unrelenting disappointment leaves you heartsick,
but a sudden good break can turn life around.
—Proverbs 13:12

If you already have something, you don't need to hope for it.
—Romans 8:24 (NLT)

Remember when you were a child and somebody asked you what you wanted to be when you grew up? Maybe you already had a picture in your mind: You wanted to be a doctor or an astronaut or a mommy. Or all three. You wanted to be as beautiful as Cinderella with a handsome prince to match. Or you wanted to have adventures in Narnia or Neverland and not grow up for a long, long time.

You dreamed.

Do you still dream? Or have you woken up once too often to a reality so different from your dreams that you've given them up?

*The love of your life, your prince.*

*The clever, delightful, godly children you'd have together.*

*The valuable, creative work you'd contribute to a grateful world.*

*The warm church community where the people passionately care for both God and you.*

*The sweet daily intimacy with your Savior.*

Where are they?

Some of your dreams may have come true, but inevitably you have also known disappointment. Often the bigger your dreams, the bigger the disappointments.

So what do you do with disappointment? You could stop dreaming. If "unrelenting disappointment leaves you heartsick," then who needs it? If you don't want anything very strongly, you won't be disappointed. Many Christian women choose this path and call it contentment, but really it's hopelessness—the refusal to hope for anything you don't already have.

Another option is to be profoundly disappointed with life—angry or depressed.

Hopeless or angry, too many Christian women just stay busy, trying to make something of their lives, to cover up the disappointment their deepest longings set them up for.

Either way—whether you're "nice" or passionately angry, dutiful or defiant, wanting nothing or wanting everything—this Bible study is for you. And if you're one of the blessed few who are winsome, passionate, full of hope, yet excited about what you already have—and your women's group has decided to use this Bible study—we fervently hope you'll be a safe friend for your disappointed sisters to confide in.

# how to
## use this
# discussion guide

This discussion guide is meant to be completed on your own and in a small group. So before you begin, line up a discussion group. Perhaps you already participate in a women's group. That works. Maybe you know a few friends who could do coffee once a week. That works, too. Ask around. You'll be surprised how many of your coworkers, neighbors, and children's friends' mothers would be interested in a small-group study—especially a study like this that doesn't require vast biblical knowledge. A group of four to six is optimal—any bigger and one or more members will likely be shut out of discussions. Your small group can also be two. Choose a friend who isn't afraid to "tell it like it is." Make sure each person has her own copy of the book.

1. *Read* the Scripture passages and other readings in each lesson on your own. Let it all soak in. Then use the white space provided to "think out loud on paper." Note content in the readings that troubles you, inspires you, confuses you, or challenges you. Be honest. Be bold. Don't shy away from the hard things. If you don't understand the passage, say so. If you don't agree, say that, too. You may choose to go over the material in one thirty- to forty-five-minute focused session. Or perhaps you'll spend twenty minutes a day on the readings. If the book doesn't provide enough space for you to write, use a notebook or journal.

2. *Think* about what you read. Think about what you write. Always ask, "What does this mean?" and "Why does this matter?" about the readings. Compare different Bible translations. Respond to the questions we've provided. You may have a lot to say on one topic, little on another. That's okay—this isn't a test where you have to answer every question. When you're in your small group, come back to the topics that seem most significant. Let the experience of others broaden your wisdom. You'll be stretched here—called upon to evaluate whether your conclusions make sense. In community, that stretching can often be painful and sometimes even embarrassing. But your willingness to be transparent—your openness to the possibility of personal growth—will reap great rewards.

3. *Pray* as you go through the entire session: before you read a word, in the middle of your thinking process, when you get stuck on a concept or passage, and as you approach the time when you'll explore these passages and thoughts together in a small group. Pause when you need to ask God for inspiration or when you need to cry out in frustration. Speak your prayers, be silent, or write out your prayers by using the prayer starters we've provided throughout each lesson.

4. *Live.* (That's "live" as in "rhymes with give" as in "Give me something I can really use in my life.") Before you meet with your small group, complete as much of this section as you can (particularly the "What I Want to Discuss" section). Then, in your small group, ask the hard questions about what the lesson means to you. Dig deep for relevant, reachable goals. Record your real-world plan in the book. Commit to following through on these plans, and let the other women support you in doing so. Arrange some way of checking in with each other for encouragement.

5. *Follow up.* Don't let the life application drift away without action. Let other group members ask you how your plan is going and refer to previous "Live" as in "rhymes with give" sections often. Take time at the beginning of each new study to review. See how you're doing.

6. *Repeat* as necessary.

# small-group study tips

After going through each week's study on your own, it's time to sit down with others and go deeper. Here are a few thoughts on how to make the most of your small-group discussion time.

**Set ground rules.** You don't need many. Here are two:

*First*, you'll want group members to make a commitment to the entire eight-week study. A binding legal document with notarized signatures and commitments written in blood probably isn't necessary, but you know your friends best. Just remember this: Significant personal growth happens when group members spend enough time together to really get to know each other. Hit-and-miss attendance rarely allows this to occur.

*Second*, agree together that everyone's story is important. Time is a valuable commodity, so if you have an hour to spend together, do your best to give each person ample time to express concerns, pass along insights, and generally feel like a participating member of the group. Small-group discussions are not monologues. However, a one-person-dominated discussion isn't always a bad thing. Your role in a small group is not only to explore and expand your own understanding; it's also to support one another. If someone truly needs more of the floor, give it to her. There will be times when the needs of the one outweigh the needs of the many. Use good judgment and allow extra space when needed. *Your* time might be next week.

**Meet regularly.** Choose a time and place, and stick to it. No one likes showing up to Carmine's Cafe at 12:30, only to discover the meeting was moved to Salad Celebration at noon. Consistency removes stress that could otherwise frustrate discussion and subsequent personal growth. It's only eight weeks. You can do this.

**Talk openly.** If you enter this study with your Happy Christian Woman mask on, you're probably not alone. And you're not a "bad person" for your hesitation to unpack your life in front of friends or strangers. Maybe you're skeptical about the value of revealing the deepest parts of who you are to others. Maybe you're simply too afraid of what might fall out of the suitcase. You don't have to go to a place where you're uncomfortable. If you want to sit and listen, offer a few thoughts, or even express a surface level of your own pain, go ahead. But don't neglect what brings you to this place—that longing for real life and real connection. You can't ignore it away. Dip your feet in the water of brutal honesty and you may choose to dive in. There is healing here.

**Avoid fixing others.** Sometimes it's scary when another woman takes off her Happy Christian mask. We women have an instinct to want to "make it all better" for any hurting or angry person, whether child or adult. Also, we have varying levels of tolerance for other people's negativity. Please resist your mommy instinct. Give advice only when asked, and even then, use restraint.

**Stay on task.** Refrain from sharing material that falls into the "too much information" category. Don't spill unnecessary stuff, such as the sexual positions your husband prefers or the in-depth details of an argument you had with your mother. This is about discovering how *you* can be a better person.

**Support each other's growth.** That "Live" section isn't just busywork. If you're really ready for positive change—for spiritual growth—you'll want to take this section seriously. Not only should you personally be thorough as you summarize your discoveries, practical as you compose your goals, and realistic as you determine the support you need from the group, you also need to check back with the others in the group to see if they're following through. Be lovingly honest as you examine each other's "Live" section. Don't hold back—this is where the rubber meets the road. A lack of openness here may send other group members skidding off that road.

# disappointed?
# me?

## the beginning place

We start each lesson by asking you to do a sometimes-difficult thing: determine the core truths about the study topic as it relates to you today. And let's just admit up front that for a Christian woman to admit she's disappointed is practically heretical. It's so negative.

We promise that this whole book won't be negative. But there's a lot of negativity in the Bible—a lot of psalmists and prophets who rant about their disappointment on their way to hope and trust in a good God. So here we go.

First, many of us live somewhere on a continuum between these two attitudes:

> a. I know what I want. I know what I want that I don't have. I am profoundly disappointed (and maybe angry or depressed).

> b. I don't want anything very strongly. If I don't get what I want, it's no big deal. Half the time, I don't know what I want anyway. I think of this as contentment.

A very few of us are more like this:

> c. I know what I want that I don't have. My hope burns with desire, patience, and confidence, as well

as groaning, yearning, and anguish. I'm passionate
and tender as I persevere in life without some of the
things I most deeply long for.

Which of these statements, (a), (b), or (c), sounds most like you?
Or if none of them fits, how would you describe your thoughts and
feelings about what you want that you don't have? About disappointment, hope, patience, or hopelessness?

Second, take a few minutes to list things you want that you don't
have. Include new bathroom wallpaper and those cool shoes if you
like, but try to dig down to the things you really long for. What do you
yearn for from your husband, your children, your job, your church,
God, yourself? Or what did you long for years ago, when you were
young and idealistic?

If you chose (b) above, you may need to push yourself on this one.
And if you can't think of a thing you honestly want, that's okay. That's
a revelation in itself.

## read  i expected good, but evil showed up

Job 16:6-12

When I speak up, I feel no better;
   if I say nothing, that doesn't help either.
I feel worn down.
   God, you have wasted me totally—me and my family!
You've shriveled me like a dried prune,
   showing the world that you're against me.
My gaunt face stares back at me from the mirror,
   a mute witness to your treatment of me.
Your anger tears at me,
   your teeth rip me to shreds,
   your eyes burn holes in me—God, my enemy!
People take one look at me and gasp.
   Contemptuous, they slap me around
   and gang up against me.
And God just stands there and lets them do it,
   lets wicked people do what they want with me.
I was contentedly minding my business when God beat me up.
   He grabbed me by the neck and threw me around.


Job 30:20-28

I shout for help, God, and get nothing, no answer!
   I stand to face you in protest, and you give me a blank stare!
You've turned into my tormenter—
   you slap me around, knock me about.
You raised me up so I was riding high
   and then dropped me, and I crashed.
I know you're determined to kill me,
   to put me six feet under.

What did I do to deserve this?
   Did I ever hit anyone who was calling for help?

Haven't I wept for those who live a hard life,
  been heartsick over the lot of the poor?
But where did it get me?
    I expected good but evil showed up.
    I looked for light but darkness fell.
My stomach's in a constant churning, never settles down.
    Each day confronts me with more suffering.
I walk under a black cloud. The sun is gone.
    I stand in the congregation and protest.

## think

- What do you feel when you read this? (Discomfort? Relief? Boredom? Excitement?)
- If a friend said this to you, how would you respond?
- To what extent can you identify with Job?
- Job's friends told him he had no business talking about God like that, and they defended God. In the end, though, God praised Job's honesty and rebuked Job's friends (see Job 42:8). God also got in Job's face (see chapters 38–41). Why do you suppose God valued Job's honesty?

## pray

God, I feel . . .

## read   nice or passionate?

From *The Allure of Hope*, by Jan Meyers[1]

Her six-year-old eyes take in the dust specks floating through the sun streaming from the window to her little refuge. She is completely at rest. . . . She hums a tune as she envisions her hero—she can see herself completely abandoned to the pursuit of the knight who comes to release her from her castle. She is beautiful, and she waits for him. She is well occupied as she waits. He will come. She waits for her daddy to be done with his work so she can run into his strong arms. She knows what it is she waits for. She is happy and content to do so; she knows she is not forgotten. . . .

Not every girl knows freedom to this degree . . . but every woman carries inside her an echo of this winsome spirit.

Why is it just an echo? . . . We are far more disciplined than we are at rest, far more committed than winsome, far more "nice" than passionate, far more dutiful than free. Far more weary than filled with hope. . . .

So, why do we hesitate to live with such a childlike, open posture? Forgive such an obvious question. It is because we suffer. Each one of us can recall the moment when the childlike, open posture gave way to fear, disbelief, or disillusionment. Or perhaps we understand that living with childlike faith brings the subtle ache that does not go away. The groaning comes from unlimited vision of what could be.

## think

- Imagine yourself as the six-year-old in this reading. What goes through your mind?
- How easy for you is childlike hope? Why is that?
- Are you "far more 'nice' than passionate"? If so, how did you get that way?
- How has disappointment affected the way you deal with life?

## think (continued)

## pray

Father, you say you haven't forgotten me . . .

# read   whine, whine, whine

From the *Good Housekeeping* quiz "Do You Feel Too Sorry for Yourself?"
by Dr. Joyce Brothers[2]

Here are some typical setbacks. Imagine that these have hap-
pened to you, then ask yourself how likely it is that you'd
respond in the way described. For each question, also think
about whether you have a pattern of dealing with *disappointment*
in this way. Then learn what your answers indicate about your
coping potential—and how you can become more resilient.

**SCENARIO 1** You and your husband finally manage a weekend
away—and it rains the entire time. Your reaction: "But The
Weather Channel said it would be sunny."

very likely ( )   somewhat likely ( )   not at all likely ( )

**SCENARIO 2** The movie you've been dying to see is sold-out.
Your response: "Why does this always happen to me?"

very likely ( )   somewhat likely ( )   not at all likely ( )

**SCENARIO 3** You make an offer on your dream house, only to
be outbid by another buyer. A month later, you're still thinking
about the floral wallpaper you would have chosen for the dining
room.

very likely ( )   somewhat likely ( )   not at all likely ( )

**SCENARIO 4** Because you had a bad cold, you couldn't go
out for your birthday dinner. Upset and miserable, you spend 20
minutes on the phone venting to a friend.

very likely ( )   somewhat likely ( )   not at all likely ( )

**SCENARIO 5** You are making plans for a family trip when your furnace gives out, eating up most of your vacation funds. Now you don't even want to think about a holiday—or anything else.

very likely ( )   somewhat likely ( )   not at all likely ( )

**SCENARIO 6** Your coworker got the promotion you had hoped for. While you wouldn't do anything devious, you find yourself thinking about ways to make life hard for her.

very likely ( )   somewhat likely ( )   not at all likely ( )

**Your bounce-back style: What your answers reveal**

**SCENARIO 1** If you chose "very likely" or "somewhat likely"

Your indignation suggests you may feel entitled to have all of your plans work out. As Queen Victoria famously said: "We are not interested in the possibilities of defeat." But those of us who don't wear a tiara may not be able to order everything to our satisfaction. The belief that you can—that it "shouldn't" have rained—makes you highly vulnerable to staying stuck when life throws even the smallest curve. The cure: recognizing that your expectations may be unrealistic and working to be more flexible. Surely you can think of a way you and your husband could enjoy yourselves on a rainy afternoon without the kids. . . .

**SCENARIO 2** If you chose "very likely" or "somewhat likely"

Ah, the self-pity bug. It's easy to catch. The problem is, you now have a double *disappointment* to deal with: (1) the sold-out movie, and (2) the "proof" that nothing ever goes your way. But if faulty thinking has got you into this view of life, a "corrective" talk can get you out. Tell yourself that many things have worked out for you before and that they will again. Then see what else is playing at the multiplex.

**SCENARIO 3** If you chose "very likely" or "somewhat likely"

It's normal to feel depressed when you don't get what you want, but daydreaming about wallpaper (or any other detail) a month later suggests that you tend to be an obsessor. You need to get out of yourself. Make plans with friends and family. This would also be an excellent time to volunteer with a local community group.

**SCENARIO 4** If you chose "very likely" or "somewhat likely"

Sharing your *disappointment* with a friend is healthy. But chances are, after 20 minutes she'll be sick of your story—and you won't be feeling any better either. If hashing and rehashing is your tendency, try setting a time limit. But also think about why you do this. Is it just a bad habit? Or do you really feel life has handed you a raw deal? Counseling, practicing relaxation techniques, and turning to spiritual endeavors can help you regain perspective.

**SCENARIO 5** If you chose "very likely" or "somewhat likely"

After a big *disappointment*, of course you'll be sad. But if you tend to feel listless for weeks and weeks, you need to find ways to restore your energy. Try taking walks in the park, browsing in a bookstore, having a pedicure—whatever fits your idea of being good to yourself. If these don't work, a few counseling sessions can be helpful.

**SCENARIO 6** If you chose "very likely" or "somewhat likely"

Plotting revenge can feel sweet—for a moment. But if every *disappointment* leaves you thinking about ways to get back at someone, you're not going to feel chipper for long. When someone else gets the prize you wanted—like a promotion—you need to analyze what went wrong. Then you'll be able to focus on ways to change.

## think

- What does this quiz reveal about the way you deal with disappointment?
- How does this quiz advise a person like you to deal with disappointment? What do you think about that advice?
- Which is a bigger temptation for you?
    a. Minimizing huge disappointments (Why go there?)
    b. Blowing little ones out of proportion
    c. Both (The little ones make a great distraction.)
    d. Neither, because . . .

## pray

Lord, I have to admit . . .

# read   birth pangs

Romans 8:15-28

This resurrection life you received from God is not a timid,
grave-tending life. It's adventurously expectant, greeting God
with a childlike "What's next, Papa?" . . . We know who he is,
and we know who we are: Father and children. And we know
we are going to get what's coming to us—an unbelievable
inheritance! . . . The created world itself can hardly wait for what's
coming next. Everything in creation is being more or less held
back. God reins it in until both creation and all the creatures are
ready and can be released at the same moment into the glorious
times ahead. Meanwhile, the joyful anticipation deepens.

All around us we observe a pregnant creation. The difficult
times of pain throughout the world are simply birth pangs. But
it's not only around us; it's *within* us. The Spirit of God is arous-
ing us within. We're also feeling the birth pangs. These sterile
and barren bodies of ours are yearning for full deliverance. That
is why waiting does not diminish us, any more than waiting
diminishes a pregnant mother. We are enlarged in the waiting.
We, of course, don't see what is enlarging us. But the longer we
wait, the larger we become, and the more joyful our expectancy.

Meanwhile, the moment we get tired in the waiting, God's
Spirit is right alongside helping us along. If we don't know how
or what to pray, it doesn't matter. He does our praying in and for
us, making prayer out of our wordless sighs, our aching groans.
He knows us far better than we know ourselves, knows our
pregnant condition, and keeps us present before God. That's why
we can be so sure that every detail in our lives of love for God is
worked into something good.

# think

- Which is more like you?
  a. A "timid, grave-tending life"

b. "Adventurously expectant, greeting God with a childlike 'What's next, Papa?'"

- How is your life like the pregnancy that Paul (the author) describes in the passage?
- Does it help you to think of yourself as nine months pregnant and aching for the baby to come? If so, how? If not, why not?
- In what areas do you need the Holy Spirit's help for prayer?
- "Every detail in our lives of love for God is worked into something good." What, then, do we do with our aching groans and what feels like the agony of a woman in labor?

## pray

Spirit of God, I'm in labor, aching for . . .

## read   pointless

### Ecclesiastes 2:11, 16-25

Then I took a good look at everything I'd done, looked at all the sweat and hard work. But when I looked, I saw nothing but smoke. Smoke and spitting into the wind. There was nothing to any of it. Nothing. . . .

It's all smoke, nothing but smoke. The smart and the stupid both disappear out of sight. In a day or two they're both forgotten. Yes, both the smart and the stupid die, and that's it.

I hate life. As far as I can see, what happens on earth is a bad business. It's smoke—and spitting into the wind.

And I hated everything I'd accomplished and accumulated on this earth. I can't take it with me—no, I have to leave it to whoever comes after me. Whether they're worthy or worthless—and who's to tell?—they'll take over the earthly results of my intense thinking and hard work. Smoke.

That's when I called it quits, gave up on anything that could be hoped for on this earth. What's the point of working your fingers to the bone if you hand over what you worked for to someone who never lifted a finger for it? Smoke, that's what it is. A bad business from start to finish. So what do you get from a life of hard labor? Pain and grief from dawn to dusk. Never a decent night's rest. Nothing but smoke.

The best you can do with your life is have a good time and get by the best you can. The way I see it, that's it—divine fate. Whether we feast or fast, it's up to God.

## think

- Why does the writer here think everything is "smoke"?
- This writer thinks "what happens on earth is a bad business." From what you read in Romans (see previous "Read" section), how would you say Paul's view of what happens on earth is similar to or different from this writer's view?

- How would you compare Paul's and this writer's views of death and what lies beyond it?
- Why do you think Ecclesiastes is in the Bible? What are we supposed to get out of it?

## pray

God, when I look at what happens on earth . . .

# LIVE

## what i want to discuss

What have you discovered this week that you definitely want to discuss with your small group? Write that here. Then begin your small-group discussion with these thoughts.

## so what?

Use the following space to summarize the truths you uncovered about disappointment, how you feel about those truths, and where you need to begin in dealing with your situation. Review your "Beginning Place" if you need to remember where you began. How does God's truth affect the next step in your journey?

## now what?

What is one practical thing you can do to respond to what you discovered? What concrete action can you take? Remember to think realistically—an admirable but unreachable goal is as good as no goal. Discuss your goal in your small group to further define it.

## how?

How can your group—or even one other person—help you follow through with the goal you described? What support do you need? How will you measure the success of your plan? Write the details here.

# the man of my dreams

## a reminder:

*Before you dive into this study, spend a little time reviewing what you wrote in the previous lesson's "Live" section. How are you doing? Check with your small-group members and review your progress toward your goals. If necessary, adjust your goals and plans, and then recommit to them.*

## the beginning place

The caption reads, "Annual meeting of single, straight, employed, financially stable men with good communication skills interested in a loving and committed relationship." The picture shows a room full of empty chairs.

Been there?

If you're married to a fabulous guy, you may feel you can sit this lesson out. Don't do that. If nothing else, take this opportunity to cultivate more compassion for your less fortunate sisters and deeper gratitude for what you've got. Take a few minutes to write down the things about your man that make you skip down the sidewalk singing.

**Note:** The disappointments of marriage and singleness are different but equally painful. To honor both, the first two readings in this session offer two alternatives. You may do only the one that addresses your situation, or you may check out the brown grass on the other side of the fence. When your group gathers, be prepared to offer an open heart to someone whose situation is very different from yours.

On the other hand, if you're single and wish you weren't, or you're dating Mr. Not Quite, or you married a man who you thought was a prince but has turned out to be a frog, talk about that. What disappoints you about men—or one man in particular? What do you really, really want that you're not getting? Begin with the griping, but be prepared to go deeper.

# read  married with disappointment

From *A False Sense of Well Being*, by Jeanne Braselton[1]

When I look at my husband sitting across from me at the dining room table, calmly slicing his potatoes with the same solemn expression he might have while calculating the amortization of a loan, I am seized with a sudden desire to make grave but preposterous announcements.

*By the way, honey, I found out today I have cancer. Would you please pass the salt?*

Or, upon my collapsing to the floor, *Dear, don't let me spoil your dinner, but I believe I'm having a heart attack.*

Something tells me that even news of some medical calamity would not break his composure, that he would view it instead as the kind of situation necessitating a cool head so the proper insurance companies can be notified, the proper forms can be filed.

We have become one of those couples that spend their days moving around within the institution of marriage like the planets orbiting the sun. There is an unseen and unfelt gravitational force that keeps us locked together in our own elliptical paths, but we remain far enough away from each other so we won't collide. The space across our long, well-polished dining room table is becoming wider and wider.

## think

- In what ways do you feel like this woman? In what ways is your marriage different from hers?
- What did you hope for in your marriage when you were a new bride?
- It might be easy for you to list the things that disappoint you about your husband. Instead, try listing at least five good things about him.
- How do you deal with being disappointed in your husband? Do you:

&#9745; Yell, bicker, or make snarky comments?
&#9745; Withhold or lose interest in sex?
&#9744; Eat?
&#9744; Read romance novels or watch romantic TV and movies?
&#9745; Gripe to friends?
&#9745; Try to make yourself stop wanting more from him?
&#9745; Pray for the ache to go away?
&#9744; Other _____?

- What do you think are some good ways of dealing with disappointment in your man?
- Remember the aching groans and painful pregnancy from Romans 8 (see page 25)? Talk about how that passage is relevant to your marriage.

## pray

Father, my husband . . .

# read  single over thirty

From *Emily's Reasons Why Not*, by Carrie Gerlach[2]

I wouldn't be here [in a counselor's office] if I weren't alone. I
haven't lost touch with reality and I don't hear voices. I'm just
having trouble concentrating on anything except the chiming of
my ovaries. They're a ticking clock, telling me the game is almost
over. Time is running out. Ten . . . nine . . . eight . . .

Two men and a baseball player ago I was confident. Now
I am feeling the pressure. I may be behind, but I'm not ready
to settle for some random anyone, not ready for life of loveless,
overwhelming compromise. What I need is some good advice,
the kind you don't take chances on with friends or family. If they
had the answer I would have heard it already.

I am a professional woman. I need pro counsel. Well, *need*
seems strong. I don't *need* anyone. I am part of the generation
who *got this far.* But now, as if stripped of all defense and pre-
tense, I find no comfort in this hollow independence. And these
chiming ovaries are so loud that I can't ignore them anymore. I'm
terrified that someday soon the chiming will STOP! The buzzer
will sound. The players will leave the field. And I will be forced
to watch from the sidelines.

I'll miss the chiming that drove me nuts and be forever-
more reminded by the silence that I missed the life I *once upon
a time . . . wished upon a star . . .* I'd have. I will be never-
endingly tortured by longings of a little girl inside who doesn't
understand. . . .

# think

- In what ways do you identify with this woman? How are you
  different from her?
- If you can't have the man of your dreams, what are the qualities of a "good enough" man?

- What qualities in a man are "reasons why not" for you—
  reasons not to get involved?
- Remember the aching groans and painful pregnancy from
  Romans 8 (see page 25)? Talk about how that passage is
  relevant to your singleness.

## pray

When I think about praying with a childlike "What's next, Papa?" . . .

## read   if only jesus were available

Ephesians 5:21-33

> Out of respect for Christ, be courteously reverent to one another.
> Wives, understand and support your husbands in ways that show your support for Christ. The husband provides leadership to his wife the way Christ does to his church, not by domineering but by cherishing. So just as the church submits to Christ as he exercises such leadership, wives should likewise submit to their husbands.
> Husbands, go all out in your love for your wives, exactly as Christ did for the church—a love marked by giving, not getting. Christ's love makes the church whole. His words evoke her beauty. Everything he does and says is designed to bring the best out of her, dressing her in dazzling white silk, radiant with holiness. And that is how husbands ought to love their wives. They're really doing themselves a favor—since they're already "one" in marriage.
> No one abuses his own body, does he? No, he feeds and pampers it. That's how Christ treats us, the church, since we are part of his body. And this is why a man leaves father and mother and cherishes his wife. No longer two, they become "one flesh." This is a huge mystery, and I don't pretend to understand it all. What is clearest to me is the way Christ treats the church. And this provides a good picture of how each husband is to treat his wife, loving himself in loving her, and how each wife is to honor her husband.

## think

- How does Paul's exhortation to husbands compare to what you long for from your husband (or from a husband, if you're single)?
- Is your husband trying to be the man Paul describes? How's he doing?

- What do you think you should do if your husband isn't trying?
- Reflect on what Paul says about Christ's love for the church, including you. What do you feel? How does this affect the way you deal with your marriage or your single state?
- If you're married, what is one thing you can do to be more like the wife Paul describes?

## pray

Christ, your love . . .

## read    to be completely frank

From the *Today's Christian Woman* article "The Toughest Questions Singles Ask," by Virginia McInerney[3]

A while ago the Lord began to deal with me about my own anger toward him over my singleness. Frustration had been building inside me, and I wanted to blame God. After all, in his sovereignty, this was what he'd chosen, or allowed, for me—and I didn't like it. I knew I had to admit to my anger, but I was afraid to do so. I thought, *I can't express that to God . . . I mean, this is* God *we're talking about! I can't yell at him.*

But then one day several things in my life went wrong in rapid succession, and I blew up. As I drove to a church seminar, of all things, I started to yell at God. Between my angry words, I apologized, "I'm sorry I feel this way. You have every right to strike me with a bolt of lightning. But this is how I feel."

The Bible says God desires truth in our innermost being (Psalm 51:6). Finally I was telling God the truth about how I felt. Even though I was seeing the situation in a wrong light, it had to come up and out, since God is the only one who could right my thinking and diffuse my anger. By stuffing my anger inside, I'd really been turning my back on him.

I'm not condoning anger with God. But we can't just pretend it isn't there. We can't make it go away by a sheer act of will. Acknowledging it by being honest is the starting point. Confession follows. Then God forgives us and cleanses us (1 John 1:9).

Great people of faith—such as Moses, Job, and David—experienced anger toward God, too. Thankfully, he understands our humanity, and he's merciful.

## think

- What do you think about yelling at God?
- Are you angry at God about anything? If so, what?

- How easy is it for you to tell God what you really think and feel? Why is that?

## pray

God, the truth is . . .

# read   happily ever after?

From the *Books and Culture* article "When Marriage Brings Suffering," by David P. Gushee[4]

People need to be taught, as they were in more sober times, that a measure of suffering is an inevitable feature of marriage. Swept away by the candlelight-and-roses vision of marriage promoted by every bride's magazine on the newsstand, we have misplaced this homely truth. Even Christians, whose doctrine of sin ought to help us know better, have forgotten to teach that marriage will not just fail to prevent suffering but actually brings suffering our way. "Not only does marriage fail to mitigate the struggles of life . . . it actually deepens them, rendering them even more poignant, because [it's] more personal."[5]

Many Christians have joined their societal compatriots in seeking relief from suffering through divorce. Sometimes they offer little evidence that they have considered what the Bible really says about suffering itself. This is a great tragedy. It has led to the unnecessary destruction of many marriages and the collapse of Christian credibility on this issue. . . .

Because human beings are imperfect sinners, we all fall short of fulfilling [marital] promises in all their potential. Falling short in a way that can be expected of normal sinful human beings is not grounds for divorce. However, situations emerge in which a pattern develops of willful and repeated violations of both the letter and the spirit of such promises. . . .

It is obvious that a pattern of physical and emotional abuse, the steady refusal of conjugal relations, the willful mistreatment or abuse of the couple's children, the refusal to contribute any effort to shared family labors either paid or unpaid, and the creation of an environment of unremitting hostility or hatred are all examples of violations of the covenant promises made on the wedding day. The circumstances in which such promise-breaking could create sufficient suffering to morally justify divorce cannot be determined by way of a general statement, but certainly such circumstances exist.

## think

- If you are or were married, did you go into it expecting that "a measure of suffering is an inevitable feature of marriage"? Describe your expectations.
- If you're single, what kinds of suffering in marriage would you reasonably expect?
- What are the sources of suffering in your marriage?
- Do you think about divorce as a solution to your marital disappointments? If so, how does this reading affect you?
- In what ways do you agree or disagree with this reading?

## pray

Lord, my suffering . . .

# read   let's give suffering a big hug!

Luke 9:23-26

Then he [Jesus] told them what they could expect for themselves: "Anyone who intends to come with me has to let me lead. You're not in the driver's seat—I am. Don't run from suffering; embrace it. Follow me and I'll show you how. Self-help is no help at all. Self-sacrifice is the way, *my* way, to finding yourself, your true self. What good would it do to get everything you want and lose you, the real you? If any of you is embarrassed with me and the way I'm leading you, know that the Son of Man will be far more embarrassed with you when he arrives in all his splendor in company with the Father and the holy angels."

## think

- How has suffering affected the way you relate to men, or to your husband in particular?
- What do you think it means to embrace suffering in a positive way?
- What does good, healthy self-sacrifice look like for you in your relationships with men (if you're single) or your husband (if you're married)?
- We women have a long history of sacrificing. Many would argue that we sometimes lose our true selves in the process. What do you think Jesus would say about this?

## pray

Jesus, I want to let you lead, but . . .

# LIVE

## what i want to discuss

What have you discovered this week that you definitely want to discuss with your small group? Write that here. Then begin your small-group discussion with these thoughts.

## so what?

Use the following space to summarize the truths you uncovered about your marriage or singleness, how you feel about those truths, and where you need to begin in dealing with your situation. Review your "Beginning Place" if you need to remember where you began. How does God's truth affect the next step in your journey?

## now what?

What is one practical thing you can do to respond to what you discovered? What concrete action can you take? Remember to think realistically—an admirable but unreachable goal is as good as no goal. Discuss your goal in your small group to further define it.

## how?

How can your group—or even one other person—help you follow through with the goal you described? What support do you need? How will you measure the success of your plan? Write the details here.

# my glamorous career

## a reminder:

*Before you dive into this study, spend a little time reviewing what you wrote in the previous lesson's "Live" section. How are you doing? Check with your small-group members and review your progress toward your goals. If necessary, adjust your goals and plans, and then recommit to them.*

## the beginning place

Women of our generation have many more options for our life's work than women did a century ago. We can choose to be full-time wives and mothers; become full-time doctors, firefighters, politicians, painters; or have both families and careers.

*Theoretically.*

Reality for many of us is different. Maybe we want to be full-time moms, but life has denied us children or our families need our income from a paying job; or we lacked the time and money to get the schooling our dream career required; or we entered what we hoped would be an exciting field, only to find it drudgery. Juggling a job and a family may be bleeding us dry, or we've been downsized, outsourced, or reengineered into a low-wage dead end.

We're not all miserable—far from it—but many of us carry disappointment that what we do all day isn't what we wish it were. Some of us are bitter. Others have made peace with our lot by numbing our dreams, but the anesthesia has spread through our souls and left us dutiful, committed, passionless shadows. Sheer weariness may take the shine off even the brightest life.

What's your story? As you begin today, write about your job—paid or unpaid. What do you love about it? What do you not love? What do you long for, or what did you long for once upon a time?

# read   if only . . .

From *Secret Longings of the Heart*, by Carol Kent[1]

- "I'm thirty-two years old and I'm still trying to figure out what I want to be when I grow up! Being single doesn't allow me the buffer of another person helping with household expenses while I investigate other job opportunities. I long to be in a work or ministry situation that will allow me to fully develop my potential. My deepest desire is to be all that I can be. I know I have potential that hasn't been tapped yet. I'm locked in a dead-end job because I'm afraid to risk failure—and bankruptcy! What should I do?" . . .

- "I just passed the bar exam this year. My parents sacrificed to put me through undergraduate school and then law school. My husband has a good job—nothing close to my earning potential—but his employment does meet our basic living expenses and a little more. Now that I'm the mother of two small children, becoming a practicing attorney has lost its appeal. I believe there's nothing more important I could do right now than be with my kids, but I'm feeling tremendous pressure because of my parents' expectations. They can't understand why I would consider wasting all of that time and money on my education if I'm not going to use it. Are my desires wrong?" . . .

- "I feel trapped. I married at eighteen, had four children by the time I was twenty-five, and have never had an opportunity to go to college. When I'm with a group of women like you, I feel inadequate."

## think

- How is your story like or unlike those in this reading?
- When you were in your early twenties, what did you hope for from your life's work?

- How do you deal with the gap between what is and what might have been?
- Do you ever envy other women? If so, what do they have that you envy?
- Do you ever feel that what you do all day is less important than what someone else does? If so, what is it about your daily work that seems unimportant?

## pray

Lord, I long for . . .

# read  the fall of work

**Genesis 2:15-18; 3:8-13,16-19**

God took the Man and set him down in the Garden of Eden to work the ground and keep it in order.

God commanded the Man, "You can eat from any tree in the garden, except from the Tree-of-Knowledge-of-Good-and-Evil. Don't eat from it. The moment you eat from that tree, you're dead.

God said, "It's not good for the Man to be alone; I'll make him a helper, a companion." . . .

When they heard the sound of God strolling in the garden in the evening breeze, the Man and his Wife hid in the trees of the garden, hid from God.

God called to the Man: "Where are you?"

He said, "I heard you in the garden and I was afraid because I was naked. And I hid."

God said, "Who told you you were naked? Did you eat from that tree I told you not to eat from?"

The Man said, "The Woman you gave me as a companion, she gave me fruit from the tree, and, yes, I ate it."

God said to the Woman, "What is this that you've done?"

"The serpent seduced me," she said, "and I ate." . . .

He [God] told the Woman:
"I'll multiply your pains in childbirth;
     you'll give birth to your babies in pain.
You'll want to please your husband,
     but he'll lord it over you."

He told the Man:
"Because you listened to your wife
     and ate from the tree
That I commanded you not to eat from,
     "Don't eat from this tree,'

The very ground is cursed because of you;
> getting food from the ground
Will be as painful as having babies is for your wife;
> You'll be working in pain all your life long.
The ground will sprout thorns and weeds,
> You'll get your food the hard way,
Planting and tilling and harvesting,
> sweating in the fields from dawn to dusk,
Until you return to that ground yourself, dead and buried;
> you started out as dirt, you'll end up dirt."

## think

- Before the first man and woman sinned, work was already part of God's plan for them. They had to care for the garden. How is work in a fallen world different from what it would have been like if humans had never sinned?
- How did sin affect the woman's roles as wife and mother?
- How did sin affect the work of getting food for the family?
- Where do you see these effects of human fallenness in your situation as wife, mother, single woman, and/or paid worker?

## pray

Father, you made me to share in the work of running this garden, but . . .

# read a tough job

Nehemiah 4:1-23

*Nehemiah became governor of the Jews in Judah under intense opposition from leaders of other ethnic groups. He was determined to rebuild the ruined wall of Jerusalem, despite harassment from his enemies.*

When Sanballat heard that we were rebuilding the wall he exploded in anger, vilifying the Jews. In the company of his Samaritan cronies and military he let loose: "What are these miserable Jews doing? Do they think they can get everything back to normal overnight? Make building stones out of make-believe?"

At his side, Tobiah the Ammonite jumped in and said, "That's right! What do they think they're building? Why, if a fox climbed that wall, it would fall to pieces under his weight."

Nehemiah prayed, "Oh listen to us, dear God. We're so despised: Boomerang their ridicule on their heads; have their enemies cart them off as war trophies to a land of no return; don't forgive their iniquity, don't wipe away their sin—they've insulted the builders!"

We kept at it, repairing and rebuilding the wall. The whole wall was soon joined together and halfway to its intended height because the people had a heart for the work.

When Sanballat, Tobiah, the Arabs, the Ammonites, and the Ashdodites heard that the repairs of the walls of Jerusalem were going so well—that the breaks in the wall were being fixed—they were absolutely furious. They put their heads together and decided to fight against Jerusalem and create as much trouble as they could. We countered with prayer to our God and set a round-the-clock guard against them.

But soon word was going around in Judah,

The builders are pooped,
    the rubbish piles up;

We're in over our heads,
we can't build this wall.

And all this time our enemies were saying, "They won't
know what hit them. Before they know it we'll be at their throats,
killing them right and left. *That* will put a stop to the work!"
The Jews who were their neighbors kept reporting, "They have
us surrounded; they're going to attack!" If we heard it once, we
heard it ten times.

So I stationed armed guards at the most vulnerable places of the
wall and assigned people by families with their swords, lances, and
bows. After looking things over I stood up and spoke to the nobles,
officials, and everyone else: "Don't be afraid of them. Put your
minds on the Master, great and awesome, and then fight for your
brothers, your sons, your daughters, your wives, and your homes."

Our enemies learned that we knew all about their plan and
that God had frustrated it. And we went back to the wall and
went to work. From then on half of my young men worked while
the other half stood guard with lances, shields, bows, and mail
armor. Military officers served as backup for everyone in Judah
who was at work rebuilding the wall. The common laborers
held a tool in one hand and a spear in the other. Each of the
builders had a sword strapped to his side as he worked. I kept
the trumpeter at my side to sound the alert.

Then I spoke to the nobles and officials and everyone else:
"There's a lot of work going on and we are spread out all along
the wall, separated from each other. When you hear the trumpet
call, join us there; our God will fight for us."

And so we kept working, from first light until the stars came
out, half of us holding lances.

I also instructed the people, "Each person and his helper is
to stay inside Jerusalem—guards by night and workmen by day."

We all slept in our clothes—I, my brothers, my workmen,
and the guards backing me up. And each one kept his spear in
his hand, even when getting water.

## think

- What do you think of the way Nehemiah prays about his enemies?
- Nehemiah deals with the challenges of his job with a combination of tough, practical action and prayer. How do you deal with the challenges of your work?
- What, if anything, can you learn from the way Nehemiah handles his job? Or is his approach too masculine for you?
- When the workers grow discouraged, Nehemiah says, "Don't be afraid of them. Put your minds on the Master, great and awesome." What do you fear? When you put your mind on the Master, what thoughts and feelings arise?

## pray

Great and awesome Master, the challenges of my work . . .

## read bringing joy to the job

From *Finding Flow*, by Mihaly Csikszentmihalyi[2]

A concrete example may illustrate best what I mean by leading a good life. Years ago my students and I studied a factory where railroad cars were assembled. The main workplace was a huge, dirty hangar where one could hardly hear a word because of the constant noise. Most of the welders who worked there hated their jobs and were constantly watching the clock in anticipation of quitting time. As soon as they were out of the factory they hurried to the neighborhood saloons or took a drive across the state line for more lively action.

Except for one of them. The exception was Joe, a barely literate man in his sixties, who had trained himself to understand and to fix every piece of equipment in the factory, from cranes to computer monitors. He loved to take on machinery that didn't work, figure out what was wrong with it, and set it right again. At home, he and his wife built a large rock garden on two empty lots next to their house, and in it he built misty fountains that made rainbows—even at night. The hundred or so welders who worked at the same plant respected Joe, even though they couldn't quite make him out. They asked his help whenever there was a problem. Many claimed that without Joe the factory might just as well close.

## think

- How did Joe turn a lousy job into a life well lived?
- What attitudes—about oneself, about others, about life—does it take to be a Joe?
- Joe found a way to use his talent (building things) to do work that pleased God—work that provided for his family, created beauty, and made others' lives better. What talents do you have? What do you love to do? If you don't know, how can you find out?

- What in your workplace needs to be done well? How can you contribute to doing it?
- How was Joe's contentment different from the kind of contentment that comes from not wanting much?

# pray

Father, what I love to do . . .

## read   does it really make a difference?

### Ecclesiastes 3:9-14

But in the end, does it really make a difference what anyone does? I've had a good look at what God has given us to
do—busywork, mostly. True, God made everything beautiful
in itself and in its time—but he's left us in the dark, so we can
never know what God is up to, whether he's coming or going.
I've decided that there's nothing better to do than go ahead and
have a good time and get the most we can out of life. That's
it—eat, drink, and make the most of your job. It's God's gift.

I've also concluded that whatever God does, that's the way
it's going to be, always. No addition, no subtraction. God's done
it and that's it. That's so we'll quit asking questions and simply
worship in holy fear.

### Colossians 3:22-25

Servants, do what you're told by your earthly masters. And don't
just do the minimum that will get you by. Do your best. Work
from the heart for your real Master, for God, confident that you'll
get paid in full when you come into your inheritance. Keep in
mind always that the ultimate Master you're serving is Christ. The
sullen servant who does shoddy work will be held responsible.
Being Christian doesn't cover up bad work.

## think

- What attitudes about work does Ecclesiastes argue for? How
  are the attitudes similar and/or different from the ones in
  Colossians?
- How do your attitudes compare to Ecclesiastes? To Colossians?
- What can it look like for you to "work from the heart for your
  real Master"?

## think (continued)

## pray

Master, I want to be the kind of worker who . . .

# LIVE

## what i want to discuss

What have you discovered this week that you definitely want to discuss with your small group? Write that here. Then begin your small-group discussion with these thoughts.

## so what?

Use the following space to summarize the truths you uncovered about work, how you feel about those truths, and where you need to begin in dealing with your situation. Review your "Beginning Place" if you need to remember where you began. How does God's truth affect the next step in your journey?

## now what?

What is one practical thing you can do to respond to what you discovered? What concrete action can you take? Remember to think realistically—an admirable but unreachable goal is as good as no goal. Discuss your goal in your small group to further define it.

## how?

How can your group—or even one other person—help you follow through with the goal you described? What support do you need? How will you measure the success of your plan? Write the details here.

# my brilliant, charming children

## a reminder:

*Before you dive into this study, spend a little time reviewing what you wrote in the previous lesson's "Live" section. How are you doing? Check with your small-group members and review your progress toward your goals. If necessary, adjust your goals and plans, and then recommit to them.*

## the beginning place

The Bible is packed with stories of childless women who bear sons (they're always sons) after long years of anguished waiting. Countless women have read those stories and asked, "God, when will it happen to me? Or do I matter less to you than Sarah and Hannah?"

The Bible is also full of sons and daughters who grow up to break their parents' hearts. Raising children is one thing; raising godly and joyful adults is a whole different marathon.

So what's your situation with children? If you have them, what about them makes you grateful? What makes you angry, afraid, or sad? If you don't have them, how do you feel about that?

If you have no children, you might want to invest your time in the first and last readings and scan the others to see what seems relevant. If you have children, you might want to focus most on the second, third, fourth, and fifth readings.

**read**   oh, god, if you'll come through for me,
i'll . . .

### 1 Samuel 1:1-11

There once was a man who lived in Ramathaim. . . . His name
was Elkanah. . . . He had two wives. The first was Hannah; the
second was Peninnah. Peninnah had children; Hannah did not.

Every year this man went from his hometown up to Shiloh
to worship and offer a sacrifice to God-of-the-Angel-Armies. Eli
and his two sons, Hophni and Phinehas, served as the priests of
God there. When Elkanah sacrificed, he passed helpings from the
sacrificial meal around to his wife Peninnah and all her children,
but he always gave an especially generous helping to Hannah
because he loved her so much, and because God had not given
her children. But her rival wife taunted her cruelly, rubbing it in
and never letting her forget that God had not given her children.
This went on year after year. Every time she went to the sanctuary of God she could expect to be taunted. Hannah was reduced
to tears and had no appetite.

Her husband Elkanah said, "Oh, Hannah, why are you crying? Why aren't you eating? And why are you so upset? Am I not
of more worth to you than ten sons?"

So Hannah ate. Then she pulled herself together, slipped
away quietly, and entered the sanctuary. The priest Eli was on
duty at the entrance to God's Temple in the customary seat.
Crushed in soul, Hannah prayed to God and cried and cried—
inconsolably. Then she made a vow:

> Oh, God-of-the-Angel-Armies,
> If you'll take a good, hard look at my pain,
> If you'll quit neglecting me and go into action for me
> By giving me a son,
> I'll give him completely, unreservedly to you.
> I'll set him apart for a life of holy discipline.

## think

- If you don't have children, what have family members and other women said that has either helped or hurt you?
- What does a childless woman need to hear from her friends? What does she need them to do?
- Have you ever bargained with God? Have you ever said, "Oh, God, if you'll _____, then I'll _____"? If so, what bargain did you offer God? What have been the results so far?
- God gave Hannah a son, and she fulfilled her part of the bargain. What do you think about bargaining with God in this way?

## pray

Oh, GOD-of-the-Angel-Armies . . .

## read  molding the perfect kid

From the *Ladies' Home Journal* article "I'm Disappointed in My Daughter," by Lynn Harris[1]

Mark and I now realize that Elizabeth has been repudiating our lifestyle in every way she can. She spends her evenings in bars and pool halls. When she is angry, four-letter words just fly out of her mouth. Although art and literature are important to us, Elizabeth rarely even picks up a newspaper.

Being a mother seemed so simple when Elizabeth was a toddler. Today, I don't know what "good parenting" means anymore. If my daughter is not as "successful" as her college-graduate peers, am I suddenly a bad parent? All too often, the echo in my mind clearly whispers, yes.

At work, friends bring in pictures of their daughters in bridal gowns and talk about their children's graduate work or creative endeavors. Envious of them and sad for myself, I try to smile bravely, wishing I could brag, too. If they should ask, am I supposed to say, "I'm relieved our daughter is at least barely managing to support herself, and I'm pretty sure she wouldn't steal, lie or deliberately hurt anyone"? . . .

As I see it now, the concept that our children are clay to be molded into something we value is probably the most damaging idea we held as parents. Yes, I think Mark and I did too much guiding, too much protecting, too much hovering. However lovingly, we tried to mold her according to the inclinations of our own personalities, without regard for the fact that this child was always a separate, distinct being. I see now that Elizabeth felt the hurt of not being what we wanted her to be, and rebellion seemed the only path to finding out who she really was.

## think

- If you have children, think back to when they were babies. What did you hope for them as teens and adults? (If your children are still small, what do you hope for them?)
- Do you feel disappointed in any of your children? If so, what disappoints you?
- "The concept that our children are clay to be molded into something we value is probably the most damaging idea we held as parents." What do you think of this statement?
- Do your children feel pressure to become what you want? How can you tell?

## pray

Lord, you are my children's Creator and Master . . .

## read   god knew i needed tough kids

From *Parenting Adolescents*, by Kevin Huggins[2]

After several months of work on his own life, Mitch [a surgeon] came to a startling revelation about himself. "You know," he said, "I'm starting to understand at least part of the reason why God gave me the teenagers he did. They're tough kids, but God knew I needed tough kids to bring me to the end of myself. Before they became adolescents, I thought I had it made. In regular surgeon-style, I had everything sewn up, so much so that I didn't need God in a practical way. When my kids started to bleed, in a matter of speaking, I went to work to sew them up too. But nothing I did worked after they reached thirteen. It was the first time my mind and skills weren't enough.

"I still have no idea how my kids will turn out, but I've begun to trust the Lord for the strength and wisdom to parent them in a whole new way—a way I never knew was possible. Something had to completely shift inside of me before I could start to love them just the way they are. I think they sense something has changed in me. And I really think that's had more impact on them than anything I could have ever said or done.". . .

The kind of model Mitch shifted to is outlined in the fifth and sixth chapter of Galatians . . . one I call the ministry model of parenting. . . .

*Rather than devoting their energies to trying to change her kids' conduct, [the parent] concentrates on changing her own character.* Although her awareness and concern over her kids' character and conduct continue to grow, she understands that, apart from the Spirit of God doing a work in her own heart, she can have no constructive influence in their lives.

## think

- To what extent do you have to depend on God rather than on your own skills as a parent?
- What do you think of the idea of a parent focusing on changing her own character rather than her kids' conduct?
- How easy is it for you to love your kids the way they are? Why is that?

## pray

God, I need your help to . . .

## read spirit-led parenting

Galatians 5:16-23

Live freely, animated and motivated by God's Spirit. Then you won't feed the compulsions of selfishness. For there is a root of sinful self-interest in us that is at odds with a free spirit, just as the free spirit is incompatible with selfishness. These two ways of life are antithetical, so that you cannot live at times one way and at times another way according to how you feel on any given day. Why don't you choose to be led by the Spirit and so escape the erratic compulsions of a law-dominated existence?

It is obvious what kind of life develops out of trying to get your own way all the time: . . . a stinking accumulation of mental and emotional garbage; frenzied and joyless grabs for happiness; . . . all-consuming-yet-never-satisfied wants; a brutal temper; an impotence to love or be loved; divided homes and divided lives; small-minded and lopsided pursuits. . . . I could go on. . . .

But what happens when we live God's way? He brings gifts into our lives, much the same way that fruit appears in an orchard—things like affection for others, exuberance about life, serenity. We develop a willingness to stick with things, a sense of compassion in the heart, and a conviction that a basic holiness permeates things and people. We find ourselves involved in loyal commitments, not needing to force our way in life, able to marshal and direct our energies wisely.

## think

- Paul criticizes people who want to get their own way all the time. How is this relevant to parenting? For instance, is Paul saying that parents shouldn't have rules?
- How should a parent go about following the lead of the Holy Spirit?
- What do you think the Holy Spirit currently wants to do in your heart?

- Some parents seem driven to make their kids turn out okay so that they, the parents, won't feel like failures. What do you think Paul would say about a parent who is driven by a fear of failure?

# pray

Holy Spirit, I want to follow your lead . . .

**read**   you think *your* family is dysfunctional?

2 Samuel 13:1-2,6-7,14-15,18-23,28-29,37

Absalom, David's son, had a sister who was very attractive. Her name was Tamar. Amnon, also David's son, was in love with her. Amnon was obsessed with his sister Tamar to the point of making himself sick over her. . . .

So Amnon took to his bed and acted sick. When the king came to visit, Amnon said, "Would you do me a favor? Have my sister Tamar come and make some nourishing dumplings here where I can watch her and be fed by her." . . .

David sent word to Tamar who was home at the time: "Go to the house of your brother Amnon and prepare a meal for him." . . .

Being much stronger than she, he raped her.

No sooner had Amnon raped her than he hated her—an immense hatred. The hatred that he felt for her was greater than the love he'd had for her. "Get up," he said, "and get out!" . . .

She was wearing a long-sleeved gown. (That's how virgin princesses used to dress from early adolescence on.) Tamar poured ashes on her head, then she ripped the long-sleeved gown, held her head in her hands, and walked away, sobbing as she went.

Her brother Absalom said to her, "Has your brother Amnon had his way with you? Now, my dear sister, let's keep it quiet—a family matter. He is, after all, your brother. Don't take this so hard." Tamar lived in her brother Absalom's home, bitter and desolate.

King David heard the whole story and was enraged, but he didn't discipline Amnon. David doted on him because he was his firstborn. Absalom quit speaking to Amnon—not a word, whether good or bad—because he hated him for violating his sister Tamar.

Two years went by. One day Absalom threw a sheep-shearing party in Baal Hazor in the vicinity of Ephraim and invited all the king's sons. . . .

Absalom prepared a banquet fit for a king. Then he instructed his servants, "Look sharp, now. When Amnon is well into the sauce and feeling no pain, and I give the order 'Strike Amnon,' kill him. And don't be afraid—I'm the one giving the command. Courage! You can do it!"

Absalom's servants did to Amnon exactly what their master ordered. . . .

David mourned the death of his son a long time.

## think

- Before this story took place, David had seduced a married woman and then murdered the woman's husband. His sons knew that. How might David's actions have affected his sons' beliefs and actions?
- How important was it for David to examine his own character when his sons did wrong? What makes you say that?
- Does your guilt influence the way you deal with your kids? How do you think a parent should handle his or her guilt?
- Do you identify with Tamar's story? If so, how can your group care for you?

## pray

Father, I confess . . .

**read**   the queen of low expectations

From the *Good Housekeeping* article "You Can Get Over Disappointment," by Judith Newman[3]

The real reason I'm rarely disappointed is that I'm the Queen of Low Expectations. A close friend gossips about me behind my back? Eh, what can you do? People talk; it's human nature. My husband refuses to go on vacation with me after I'd been looking forward to a break for months? Well, I knew he was moody when I married him; why should I expect him to change? . . . If you never want anything too badly, you'll never be disappointed: That's always been my motto.

So when a *disappointment* finally hit—and, granted, it was a big one—I wasn't prepared. What do you mean I can't get pregnant? . . .

Once married, I tried for several years to conceive, but without success. Then I went to an infertility specialist, got pregnant, was smug for about 30 seconds—and had an early miscarriage. I was startled by how let down I felt. After all, I'd only been pregnant a couple of weeks. And if I were really honest with myself, I wasn't even sure I wanted children. I had waited until I was a—well, the happy term the doctors use is geriatric mother. So why should I have been so surprised that I miscarried?

But I was surprised—and sad too. It doesn't matter what your intellect tells you: The moment a woman hears she's pregnant, she's mulling over which color her child will look better in: the black of the robe he'll be wearing as Supreme Court justice or the white of the lab coat she'll don while she cures cancer.

The second time I miscarried, I was more than disappointed; I was almost incapacitated by grief. The third time was another surprise: I didn't react much at all. My life had been easy; who was I to think the universe owed me all this and a child too? I would be fine, just fine. OK, I could see that some people might have thought I was upset when I brought home, unannounced, a 120-pound dog from a shelter, particularly since my husband is allergic. But I knew I was fine. Who . . . cares about children? I asked myself. They're so . . . sticky.

That was truly the low point. If being disappointed was terrible, not being disappointed was worse. Because if I wasn't disappointed, I realized, I had lost hope.

I'm not suggesting we should be pleased when we have to endure life's letdowns. (Hey, that's the second year in a row my husband forgot our anniversary! Maybe he'll forget again next year, and we'll go for the trifecta!) But we have to understand *disappointment* for what it is: a sign of our humanity, of our ability to look into the future and imagine something better for ourselves. We are disappointed only to the extent that we dream. And we all want to dream.

## think

- "We are disappointed only to the extent that we dream." Do you tend to have big dreams or small ones?
- Are some disappointments harder for you than others? If so, which ones? Why do you suppose they're harder?
- Would you like to be a person who dreams big, or one with low expectations? Why?

## pray

Lord, I want . . .

# LIVE

## what i want to discuss

What have you discovered this week that you definitely want to discuss with your small group? Write that here. Then begin your small-group discussion with these thoughts.

## so what?

Use the following space to summarize the truths you uncovered about yourself as a parent or as a woman without children, how you feel about those truths, and where you need to begin in dealing with your situation. Review your "Beginning Place" if you need to remember where you began. How does God's truth affect the next step in your journey?

## now what?

What is one practical thing you can do to respond to what you discovered? What concrete action can you take? Remember to think realistically—an admirable but unreachable goal is as good as no goal. Discuss your goal in your small group to further define it.

## how?

How can your group—or even one other person—help you follow through with the goal you described? What support do you need? How will you measure the success of your plan? Write the details here.

# my on-fire church

## a reminder:

*Before you dive into this study, spend a little time reviewing what you wrote in the previous lesson's "Live" section. How are you doing? Check with your small-group members and review your progress toward your goals. If necessary, adjust your goals and plans, and then recommit to them.*

## the beginning place

About twenty-three million Americans claim they have made a personal commitment to Jesus Christ that is still important in their lives today yet don't go to church.[1] It seems that for a lot of born-again Christians, church is a disappointment.

And millions more Americans regularly attend churches they're not thrilled with. Just as husbands, children, and jobs let us down, so, too, do pastors, Sunday school teachers, worship leaders, and fellow members—even small groups.

As we do with our jobs and families, some of us loudly gripe about our churches, while others silently bear them or silently leave. This session is an opportunity for you to explore the roots of your feelings about church and seek a constructive way forward. If you tend to be a complainer, you might want to focus on constructive solutions. If you tend to be the queen of low expectations, allow yourself to feel what you really long for in a community of believers.

So where do you begin? Take a few minutes to write down how

you feel about church in general and your current church (if any) in particular. Discuss good points, bad points—whatever is on your mind.

## read  it's the people

From the *Christianity Today* article "Why I Return to the Pews," by John Koessler[2]

Down through the years I have made a surprising discovery. Most of the Christians I know are disappointed with their churches, finding them either too traditional or too modern. Their sermons are too theological or not theological enough. The people are cliquish. In the end, the root problem is always the same. It's the people.

Yet Sunday after Sunday these believers return to their pews, expecting God to meet them there once again. Some might view such attendance as an act of futility or an exercise in wishful thinking. I believe it is a work of grace.

The author of *The Message* and veteran pastor Eugene Peterson has written that when we get serious about the Christian life, we usually find ourselves in a place and among people that we find incompatible. "That place and people," Peterson explains, "is often called a church. It's hard to get over the disappointment that God, having made an exception in my case, doesn't call nice people to repentance."

## think

- Do you go to church? Why or why not?
- What do you long for from a community of believers?
- What to you is a "good enough" church or Christian community—good enough for you to participate in?
- Do you think it's reasonable to expect the people in churches to be nicer? What makes you say that?
- Have you ever been badly hurt by people in a church? If so, how have you dealt with that?

**think** (continued)

**pray**

Father, I long for . . .

# read   those darn thistles

Matthew 13:24-30

[Jesus] told another story. "God's kingdom is like a farmer who planted good seed in his field. That night, while his hired men were asleep, his enemy sowed thistles all through the wheat and slipped away before dawn. When the first green shoots appeared and the grain began to form, the thistles showed up, too.

"The farmhands came to the farmer and said, 'Master, that was clean seed you planted, wasn't it? Where did these thistles come from?'

"He answered, 'Some enemy did this.'

"The farmhands asked, 'Should we weed out the thistles?'

"He said, 'No, if you weed the thistles, you'll pull up the wheat, too. Let them grow together until harvest time. Then I'll instruct the harvesters to pull up the thistles and tie them in bundles for the fire, then gather the wheat and put it in the barn.'"

## think

- Why does God let thistles grow among the wheat?
- How is this story relevant to the disappointing aspects of churches?
- Does this story say anything to you about a church situation you face? If so, what?
- Many Christians move from church to church, searching for a community that will feed them. What do you think about that practice? If you've done it, talk about why.

**think** (continued)

**pray**

God, those thistles . . .

# read   something died, something came to life

From the *Christianity Today* article "The Church — Why Bother?" by Tim Stafford[3]

A friend of mine (I'll call her Lillian) joined an ordinary church. She felt comfortable there because the people were friendly. It was a good fit for her and her family. Except for the pastor.

The pastor was not a bad man — in fact, he was a good man — but Lillian realized that he held back the church. Early in his ministry he had experienced an ugly split in the church he led. The incident had marked him. At bottom he was afraid. He had to keep control, he thought — and so he stifled any initiative. He feared putting himself on the point, so he operated by manipulation.

A consistent pattern showed itself: a new lay leader would appear, would optimistically rally the church toward new ministry, and then eventually — worn out by the pastor's style of indirection and manipulation — would quit the church and go elsewhere. . . .

Lillian sometimes thought that if the pastor had been a bad man, had acted in an obviously sinful way, they might have gotten rid of him. As it was, she realized he would never leave. He had at least a decade before retirement. That began to seem like a life sentence. . . .

But Lillian does not leave churches, unless it is for a much better reason than frustration with a pastor's leadership style. She stayed. She worked. She found places where she could make a difference. And she suffered. She felt deeply the gap between what her church should be and what it actually was. It took, indeed, almost 20 long years before the pastor finally sank into retirement.

Looking back now, many years later still, Lillian finds that she cannot think a negative thought about those years and her choice to stay. It was like having a baby, she thinks. However difficult, she would not trade the experience or the result. Something died in her, but something also came to life. That something was Christ.

## think

- Lillian says her experience with the disappointing pastor killed something in her. What do you think died? What do you think she means when she says Christ came to life?
- Would you stick with a church like Lillian's? Why or why not?
- If you've stuck with a disappointing church, why have you stayed? What have been the results so far in your spiritual life? What about in the lives of others?
- If you've left a disappointing church, why did you leave? What have been the results for you and others?

## pray

Lord Jesus, I want to experience you in your death . . .

# read  why are christians so mean?

### 1 Corinthians 1:10-13

I have a serious concern to bring up with you, my friends, using the authority of Jesus, our Master. I'll put it as urgently as I can: You *must* get along with each other. You must learn to be considerate of one another, cultivating a life in common.

I bring this up because some from Chloe's family brought a most disturbing report to my attention—that you're fighting among yourselves! I'll tell you exactly what I was told: You're all picking sides, going around saying, "I'm on Paul's side," or "I'm for Apollos," or "Peter is my man," or "I'm in the Messiah group."

I ask you, "Has the Messiah been chopped up in little pieces so we can each have a relic all our own? Was Paul crucified for you? Was a single one of you baptized in Paul's name?"

### From *Renovation of the Heart*, by Dallas Willard[4]

[O]ne of the most helpful and profound statements I have read in recent years for the understanding of contemporary church life is by Leith Anderson. He notes,

> While the New Testament speaks often about churches, it is surprisingly silent about many matters that we associate with church structure and life. There is no mention of architecture, pulpits, length of typical sermons [or sermons!], rules for having a Sunday school. Little is said about style of music, order of worship, or times of church gatherings. There were no Bibles, denominations, camps, pastor's conferences, or board meeting minutes. Those who strive to be New Testament churches must seek to live its principles and absolutes, not reproduce the details.[5]

Those details simply aren't given.

Now you might ask yourself, *Why does the New Testament say nothing about all those matters to which the usual congregation today devotes almost all its thoughts and effort?* Answer: Because those matters are not primary and will take care of themselves with little attention whenever what is primary is appropriately cared for. Pay attention to the "principles and absolutes" of the New Testament church and, one might suppose, everything else will fall into place—in large part because "everything else" really doesn't matter much one way or the other. . . .

The leader of one denomination recently said to me, "When I am finished with this job I am going to write a book on the topic *Why Are Christians So Mean?*

Well, there actually is an answer to that question. And we must face this answer and effectively deal with it or Satan will sustain his stranglehold on spiritual transformation in local congregations. Christians are routinely taught by example and word that it is more important to be right (always in terms of their beloved [way of doing things] or tradition) than it is to be Christlike. In fact, being right licenses you to be mean and, indeed, *requires* you to be mean—righteously mean, of course. You must be hard on people who are wrong, and especially if they are in positions of Christian leadership. They deserve nothing better.

## think

- In the reading from 1 Corinthians, why do you think Paul is so vehement about members of a Christian community getting along with each other?
- Do people in your church fight? If so, what do they fight about? How do they fight?
- What do you make of the fact that the New Testament says little or nothing about the things Leith Anderson lists in the second reading?

- What are some of the "principles and absolutes" that you think a church should focus on?
- How important is it for you to be right? How do you feel and act when you disagree with people at church or in the wider Christian community?
- What is a Christlike way of standing up for what you believe? What ways are not Christlike?

## pray

Lord, please help me get along with . . .

## read keeping score

Matthew 18:21-35

At that point Peter got up the nerve to ask, "Master, how many times do I forgive a brother or sister who hurts me? Seven?"

Jesus replied, "Seven! Hardly. Try seventy times seven.

"The kingdom of God is like a king who decided to square accounts with his servants. As he got under way, one servant was brought before him who had run up a debt of a hundred thousand dollars. He couldn't pay up, so the king ordered the man, along with his wife, children, and goods, to be auctioned off at the slave market.

"The poor wretch threw himself at the king's feet and begged, 'Give me a chance and I'll pay it all back.' Touched by his plea, the king let him off, erasing the debt.

"The servant was no sooner out of the room when he came upon one of his fellow servants who owed him ten dollars. He seized him by the throat and demanded, 'Pay up. Now!'

"The poor wretch threw himself down and begged, 'Give me a chance and I'll pay it all back.' But he wouldn't do it. He had him arrested and put in jail until the debt was paid. When the other servants saw this going on, they were outraged and brought a detailed report to the king.

"The king summoned the man and said, 'You evil servant! I forgave your entire debt when you begged me for mercy. Shouldn't you be compelled to be merciful to your fellow servant who asked for mercy?' The king was furious and put the screws to the man until he paid back his entire debt. And that's exactly what my Father in heaven is going to do to each one of you who doesn't forgive unconditionally anyone who asks for mercy."

## think

- What's the point of Jesus' story?
- Does forgiveness mean saying it's okay for the person to keep doing the thing that hurt you? Explain your view.
- Is there anyone (an individual, a church, a group) whom you have trouble forgiving? If so, what makes this one hard for you?
- If you've been through a process of forgiving a major hurt, talk about what the process was like and how it has affected you.

## pray

Jesus, I want to forgive . . .

# LIVE

## what i want to discuss

What have you discovered this week that you definitely want to discuss with your small group? Write that here. Then begin your small-group discussion with these thoughts.

## so what?

Use the following space to summarize the truths you uncovered about church, how you feel about those truths, and where you need to begin in dealing with your situation. Review your "Beginning Place" if you need to remember where you began. How does God's truth affect the next step in your journey?

## now what?

What is one practical thing you can do to respond to what you discovered? What concrete action can you take? Remember to think realistically—an admirable but unreachable goal is as good as no goal. Discuss your goal in your small group to further define it.

## how?

How can your group—or even one other person—help you follow through with the goal you described? What support do you need? How will you measure the success of your plan? Write the details here.

# my astounding spiritual life

## a reminder:

*Before you dive into this study, spend a little time reviewing what you wrote in the previous lesson's "Live" section. How are you doing? Check with your small-group members and review your progress toward your goals. If necessary, adjust your goals and plans, and then recommit to them.*

## the beginning place

Many of us reserve the full wrath of our disappointment for ourselves. In our minds is a statue of the perfect Me on a high pedestal—a godly, content, joyful, loving prayer warrior—and we thrash ourselves whenever we fail to measure up. We can hardly manage five minutes of prayer without our minds wandering, and when it comes to love, joy, peace, patience, and the rest of it—well, we're not exactly getting straight As.

It's so difficult to pray when we have a nagging feeling that God is disappointed with us. It's much easier to work harder at serving him or to just blow off the whole spiritual life thing entirely.

So what's the state of your spiritual life? And what thoughts and feelings rumble around in your head and stomach when you contemplate such a question? Don't panic: We'll start here, but then it gets better.

## read   what does god want?

**Micah 6:6-8**

> How can I stand up before GOD
>     and show proper respect to the high God?
> Should I bring an armload of offerings
>     topped off with yearling calves?
> Would GOD be impressed with thousands of rams,
>     with buckets and barrels of olive oil?
> Would he be moved if I sacrificed my firstborn child,
>     my precious baby, to cancel my sin?
>
> But he's already made it plain how to live, what to do,
>     what GOD is looking for in men and women.
> It's quite simple: Do what is fair and just to your neighbor,
>     be compassionate and loyal in your love,
> And don't take yourself too seriously—
>     take God seriously.

**Matthew 22:35-40**

One of their religion scholars spoke for them, posing a question they hoped would show [Jesus] up: "Teacher, which command in God's Law is the most important?"

Jesus said, "'Love the Lord your God with all your passion and prayer and intelligence.' This is the most important, the first on any list. But there is a second to set alongside it: 'Love others as well as you love yourself.' These two commands are pegs; everything in God's Law and the Prophets hangs from them."

## think

- How do your expectations of yourself compare to the qualities God wants in you according to Micah and Matthew?
- How are you doing at loving God and your neighbor?

Describe your strengths and weaknesses.

- How do you feel about yourself when you read these passages? Why?
- What is one quality described in these readings that you would most like to grow in?
- What do you believe God thinks when he looks at you?

## pray

God, when I compare myself to your words . . .

## read it's not about you

From "Shipwrecked at the Stable," by Brennan Manning[1]

One day Saint Francis and Brother Leo were walking down the road. Noticing that Leo was depressed, Francis turned and asked: "Leo, do you know what it means to be pure of heart?"

"Of course. It means to have no sins, faults or weaknesses to reproach myself for."

"Ah," said Francis, "now I understand why you're sad. We will always have something to reproach ourselves for."

"Right," said Leo. "That's why I despair of ever arriving at purity of heart."

"Leo, listen carefully to me. Don't be so preoccupied with the purity of your heart. Turn and look at Jesus. Admire him. Rejoice that he is what he is—your Brother, your Friend, your Lord and Savior. That, little brother, is what it means to be pure of heart. And once you've turned to Jesus, don't turn back and look at yourself. Don't wonder where you stand with him.

"The sadness of not being perfect, the discovery that you really are sinful, is a feeling much too human, even borders on idolatry. Focus your vision outside yourself on the beauty, graciousness and compassion of Jesus Christ. The pure of heart praise him from sunrise to sundown. Even when they feel broken, feeble, distracted, insecure and uncertain, they are able to release it into his peace. A heart like that is stripped and filled—stripped of self and filled with the fullness of God. It is enough that Jesus is Lord."

After a long pause, Leo said, "Still, Francis, the Lord demands our effort and fidelity."

"No doubt about that," replied Francis. "But holiness is not a personal achievement. It's an emptiness you discover in yourself. Instead of resenting it, you accept it and it becomes the free space where the Lord can create anew."

## think

- What do you think about the way Francis defines purity of heart?
- Do you agree that the sadness of not being perfect borders on idolatry? Why or why not?
- How easy is it for you to focus your vision outside yourself on the beauty, graciousness, and compassion of Jesus Christ? Why is that?
- How do you respond to this statement: "Holiness is not a personal achievement"?

## pray

Lord Jesus, your beauty, graciousness, and compassion . . .

## read lucky you

**Psalm 32:1-5**

> Count yourself lucky, how happy you must be—
> you get a fresh start,
> your slate's wiped clean.
>
> Count yourself lucky—
> GOD holds nothing against you
> and you're holding nothing back from him.
>
> When I kept it all inside,
> my bones turned to powder,
> my words became daylong groans.
>
> The pressure never let up;
> all the juices of my life dried up.
>
> Then I let it all out;
> I said, "I'll make a clean breast of my failures to GOD."
>
> Suddenly the pressure was gone—
> my guilt dissolved,
> my sin disappeared.

## think

- Have you ever made a clean breast of your failures to God? If so, how did that affect you? If not, what keeps you from doing that?
- How easy is it for you to think of yourself as lucky and happy because you have a clean slate? Why is that?
- What would you like to admit to God right now?

## think (continued)

## pray

God, the truth is . . .

## read guilt, inc.

From *Secret Longings of the Heart*, by Carol Kent[2]

Many of us who are active members of this exclusive "guilt-trip" club have developed a flawed belief system. Some of the myths we have come to believe are the following:

- I must be a perfect Christian.
- Everyone should love me and approve of me.
- If I am a good Christian, life should be fair.
- It's a sin to feel depressed.
- If I am living in fellowship with God, I should never feel anger toward Him or other people.
- It's my job to meet everyone's needs.
- If I feel worried, I'm a bad Christian.
- If God loved me, bad things would not happen to me.
- God will bless me with health and happiness if I work hard for Him.
- When there is so much *real* tragedy in the world, it's wrong for me to feel grief over little things.

## think

- Which, if any, of the above myths do you tend to believe?
- How do those myths affect your behavior?
- For the ones you chose, describe why they are myths (or why you think they're not myths).
- If you reject those myths, will you become a wild sinner? What makes you say that?

**think** (continued)

**pray**
Father, I want to believe . . .

## read   clay pots

2 Corinthians 4:7-9,13-18

If you only look at *us*, you might well miss the brightness. We carry this precious Message around in the unadorned clay pots of our ordinary lives. That's to prevent anyone from confusing God's incomparable power with us. As it is, there's not much chance of that. You know for yourselves that we're not much to look at. We've been surrounded and battered by troubles, but we're not demoralized; we're not sure what to do, but we know that God knows what to do; we've been spiritually terrorized, but God hasn't left our side; we've been thrown down, but we haven't broken. . . .

We're not keeping this quiet, not on your life. Just like the psalmist who wrote, "I believed it, so I said it," we say what we believe. And what we believe is that the One who raised up the Master Jesus will just as certainly raise us up with you, alive. Every detail works to your advantage and to God's glory: more and more grace, more and more people, more and more praise!

So we're not giving up. How could we! Even though on the outside it often looks like things are falling apart on us, on the inside, where God is making new life, not a day goes by without his unfolding grace. These hard times are small potatoes compared to the coming good times, the lavish celebration prepared for us. There's far more here than meets the eye. The things we see now are here today, gone tomorrow. But the things we can't see now will last forever.

## think

- Why does God choose to display his great Message through ordinary lives?
- Does anything in this passage encourage you? If so, what?
- Can you honestly say that "not a day goes by without his unfolding grace"? Why or why not?

- What would you say to a woman who can't muster the enthusiasm Paul expresses in this passage?

## pray

Master, I'm not much to look at . . .

# LIVE

## what i want to discuss

What have you discovered this week that you definitely want to discuss with your small group? Write that here. Then begin your small-group discussion with these thoughts.

## so what?

Use the following space to summarize the truths you uncovered about your spiritual life, how you feel about those truths, and where you need to begin in dealing with your situation. Review your "Beginning Place" if you need to remember where you began. How does God's truth affect the next step in your journey?

## now what?

What is one practical thing you can do to respond to what you discovered? What concrete action can you take? Remember to think realistically—an admirable but unreachable goal is as good as no goal. Discuss your goal in your small group to further define it.

## how?

How can your group—or even one other person—help you follow through with the goal you described? What support do you need? How will you measure the success of your plan? Write the details here.

# resilience

## a reminder:

*Before you dive into this study, spend a little time reviewing what you wrote in the previous lesson's "Live" section. How are you doing? Check with your small-group members and review your progress toward your goals. If necessary, adjust your goals and plans, and then recommit to them.*

## the beginning place

Resilience is the ability to bounce back. When you vacuum a new high-quality carpet, the fibers spring back into their original plush condition. Old cheap carpet, on the other hand, stays matted down. We get walked on a lot in the course of life; some of us bounce back, but some just lie there, matted down.

Why the difference? It's tempting to play the blame game, but let's not. There's neurological evidence that some people are born with more resilient brains and also that early childhood experiences affect the adult brain's resilience. So if you're easily matted down, it may not be your fault.

But God is in the business of transforming all of us into the image of his Son, and Jesus was remarkably resilient. His family, his friends, and his religious community all let him down. He allowed himself to feel the full weight of his longings and disappointment (no numbness or false contentment); he didn't harden his heart against further blows, yet he kept going.

What's your initial response to the idea of resilience? Is it a quality you understand, or one that eludes you? Do you feel proud of your resilience, or guilty for not being resilient enough? We'll start here and then go deeper.

# read   how resilient are you?

From a quiz by Al Siebert, Ph.D., in *Good Housekeeping*[1]

Rate yourself from 1 to 5 (1 = very little, 5 = very strong) on the following traits:

- Curious, ask questions, want to know how things work, experiment.
- Constantly learn from experience and from the experiences of others.
- Need and expect to have things work well for yourself and others. Take good care of yourself.
- Play with new developments, find the humor, laugh at self.
- Adapt quickly to change; highly flexible.
- Feel comfortable with inner complexity. (Trusting and cautious, sensitive and tough, unselfish and selfish, optimistic and pessimistic, etc.)
- Anticipate problems and avoid difficulties.
- Develop better self-esteem and more self-confidence every year.
- Listen well. Read others with empathy (including difficult people).
- Think up creative solutions to challenges, invent ways to solve problems. Trust intuition, hunches.
- Manage the emotional side of recovery. Grieve, honor, and let go of the past.
- Expect tough situations to work out well, keep on going. Help others, bring stability in times of uncertainty and turmoil.
- Made stronger and better by bad experiences.
- Convert misfortune into good fortune.

SCORING
60-70 HIGHLY RESILIENT
50-60 BETTER THAN MOST

40-50 LOW, BUT ADEQUATE
30-40 YOU'RE STRUGGLING
30 or under SEEK HELP!

## think

- What did you learn about yourself from this quiz?
- Which of the qualities of resilience listed in this section do you most need to develop?
- What helps you be resilient? What hinders you?

## pray

Father, I want to become . . .

# read   i need a drink

Psalm 42

A white-tailed deer drinks
     from the creek;
I want to drink God,
     deep draughts of God.
I'm thirsty for God-alive.
I wonder, "Will I ever make it—
     arrive and drink in God's presence?"
I'm on a diet of tears—
     tears for breakfast, tears for supper.
All day long
     people knock at my door,
Pestering,
     "Where is this God of yours?"

These are the things I go over and over,
     emptying out the pockets of my life.
I was always at the head of the worshiping crowd,
     right out in front,
Leading them all,
     eager to arrive and worship,
Shouting praises, singing thanksgiving—
     celebrating, all of us, God's feast!

Why are you down in the dumps, dear soul?
     Why are you crying the blues?
Fix my eyes on God—
     soon I'll be praising again.
He puts a smile on my face.
     He's my God.

When my soul is in the dumps, I rehearse
     everything I know of you,

From Jordan depths to Hermon heights,
  including Mount Mizar.
Chaos calls to chaos,
  to the tune of whitewater rapids.
Your breaking surf, your thundering breakers
  crash and crush me.
Then GOD promises to love me all day,
  sing songs all through the night!
My life is God's prayer.

Sometimes I ask God, my rock-solid God,
  "Why did you let me down?
Why am I walking around in tears,
  harassed by enemies?"
They're out for the kill, these
  tormentors with their obscenities,
Taunting day after day,
  "Where is this God of yours?"

Why are you down in the dumps, dear soul?
  Why are you crying the blues?
Fix my eyes on God—
  soon I'll be praising again.
He puts a smile on my face.
  He's my God.

## think

- How does this psalm reflect resilience?
- How do your feelings and actions reflect a deep thirst (or lack of thirst) for God?
- What does it look like for you to fix your eyes on God in your current circumstances?
- Does resilience mean pretending everything's fine? What makes you say that?

# think (continued)

# pray

God, I'm thirsty . . .

## read   never quit

Luke 18:1-8

Jesus told them a story showing that it was necessary for them to pray consistently and never quit. He said, "There was once a judge in some city who never gave God a thought and cared nothing for people. A widow in that city kept after him: 'My rights are being violated. Protect me!'

"He never gave her the time of day. But after this went on and on he said to himself, 'I care nothing what God thinks, even less what people think. But because this widow won't quit badgering me, I'd better do something and see that she gets justice—otherwise I'm going to end up beaten black and blue by her pounding.'"

Then the Master said, "Do you hear what that judge, corrupt as he is, is saying? So what makes you think God won't step in and work justice for his chosen people, who continue to cry out for help? Won't he stick up for them? I assure you, he will. He will not drag his feet. But how much of that kind of persistent faith will the Son of Man find on the earth when he returns?"

## think

- How is God like or unlike the judge in this story?
- Persistence worked for the widow. Why would or wouldn't it work for you?
- How persistent are you in praying for things you think are really important? What motivates you to quit or not quit?
- What does this story have to do with handling disappointment?

# think (continued)

# pray

Master, strengthen my faith to pray persistently for . . .

# read   my life is way worse than yours

2 Corinthians 11:23-30; 12:7-9

I've worked much harder, been jailed more often, beaten up more times than I can count, and at death's door time after time. I've been flogged five times with the Jews' thirty-nine lashes, beaten by Roman rods three times, pummeled with rocks once. I've been shipwrecked three times, and immersed in the open sea for a night and a day. In hard traveling year in and year out, I've had to ford rivers, fend off robbers, struggle with friends, struggle with foes. I've been at risk in the city, at risk in the country, endangered by desert sun and sea storm, and betrayed by those I thought were my brothers. I've known drudgery and hard labor, many a long and lonely night without sleep, many a missed meal, blasted by the cold, naked to the weather.

And that's not the half of it, when you throw in the daily pressures and anxieties of all the churches. When someone gets to the end of his rope, I feel the desperation in my bones. When someone is duped into sin, an angry fire burns in my gut.

If I have to "brag" about myself, I'll brag about the humiliations that make me like Jesus. . . .

So I wouldn't get a big head, I was given the gift of a handicap to keep me in constant touch with my limitations. Satan's angel did his best to get me down; what he in fact did was push me to my knees. No danger then of walking around high and mighty! At first I didn't think of it as a gift, and begged God to remove it. Three times I did that, and then he told me,

My grace is enough; it's all you need.
My strength comes into its own in your weakness.

## think

- Why does Paul celebrate his humiliations?
- What does this passage have to say to a woman who has been disappointed by her marriage, children, career, church, or spiritual life?
- What does it take to be a person who gets on her knees— rather than just being angry or depressed—when disappointments hit?
- What is God saying to you in this passage?

## pray

Father, your grace is enough for . . .

## read   options

From the *Redbook* article "Six Ways to Deal with Disappointment," by Debra Kent[2]

**1. Take the cosmic overview.** . . . "When things don't go as I'd expected, I always wonder what the gods have in mind for me that might be even better," says Gail Fairfield. . . . Fairfield advises trying these mantras on for size: It wasn't meant to be. One door closes, another opens. There are no accidents. Every situation offers an opportunity.

**2. Get the facts.** . . . Probe to find out why you didn't get what you wanted. This kind of investigation can be painful ("If you really want to know, you didn't get the promotion because you're just plain incompetent"), but it can also set you free.

**3. Get back in control.** Formulate a plan to get what you want next time. . . . Reschedule the romantic weekend. Schedule a meeting with your boss to make your case for a promotion. You're no longer a helpless victim of circumstance—you're a woman of action.

**4. Be kind to your inner child.** That little voice inside you keeps going waaaah and won't stop? Try being as kind to it as you would be to your own child when she's suffered what seems to her a crushing blow. . . . Acknowledge the *disappointment* and don't rush to make yourself feel better. . . . Finally, remind yourself that you have the skills to survive this setback. ("It's bad but not disastrous. I can live through this.")

**5. Stop whining.** Sometimes the swiftest way to quell *disappointment* is simply this: Tell yourself to lighten up. Say it out loud if it helps: Shut up. You'll be fine. . . .

Lamenting is how you grieve over a lost opportunity. It's the nobler response because it has a beginning, middle, and end. Eventually you move through it and go on. Whining, on the other hand, is like a hamster in a wheel. . . . It goes on and on but never gets anywhere. And it drives your friends crazy. So if you've spent two weeks dwelling on the job you weren't offered and still haven't sent out another résumé, you're probably whining. Quit it.

**6. Wait it out.** If all else fails, distract yourself for a few days and you're likely to notice that the *disappointment* has faded.

## think

- How do these ways of dealing with disappointment compare to what you see in the Bible passages in this lesson?
- Which, if any, of these ways would be helpful for you?
- Think of a disappointment in your life currently. How will you handle it? What help do you need?

## pray
Lord, I'm realizing . . .

# LIVE

## what i want to discuss

What have you discovered this week that you definitely want to discuss with your small group? Write that here. Then begin your small-group discussion with these thoughts.

## so what?

Use the following space to summarize the truths you uncovered about resilience, how you feel about those truths, and where you need to begin in dealing with your situation. Review your "Beginning Place" if you need to remember where you began. How does God's truth affect the next step in your journey?

## now what?

What is one practical thing you can do to respond to what you discovered? What concrete action can you take? Remember to think realistically—an admirable but unreachable goal is as good as no goal. Discuss your goal in your small group to further define it.

## how?

How can your group—or even one other person—help you follow through with the goal you described? What support do you need? How will you measure the success of your plan? Write the details here.

# hope

## a reminder:

*Before you dive into this study, spend a little time reviewing what you wrote in the previous lesson's "Live" section. How are you doing? Check with your small-group members and review your progress toward your goals. If necessary, adjust your goals and plans, and then recommit to them.*

## the beginning place

"Hope is not a search to find God. . . . Hope is stopping our maneuverings long enough to be found by God."[1]

There are so many ways we maneuver in the face of disappointment. We lower our expectations and try merely to survive. We demand our rights. We fade so that others won't notice us. We get busy with service projects and church committees. We live through our children or our jobs. Sometimes the most hopeful thing we can do is sit still.

When you think of the word *hope*, what goes through your mind? Does hope seem strong or weak, pale or brightly colored? Do you have a lot or not much? Talk about where you start with the idea of hope.

## read   foolish courage

From *The Allure of Hope*, by Jan Meyers[2]

Look for the courage, vision, and patience in these snapshots:

- A four-year-old child daily anticipating his June birthday . . . in February
- An eighty-seven-year-old woman praying quietly for God to allow her to come home
- A woman choosing to shed tender tears with her husband (not just in front of him), knowing he has told her how uncomfortable tears make him
- A man in a stale marriage, choosing to initiate physical intimacy with his wife when she has rebuffed such advances in the past
- A single woman investing heart and soul in the lives of both single and married friends

These snapshots reveal a glimpse of what hope looks like. Can you see how each person could be indicted as "foolish"? Can you see the courage required to enter reality? Each person was envisioning something that wasn't there yet. If you have something already, you don't need to hope for it (Romans 8:24). And can you see how hoping causes us to love in ways that would not be possible without a vision of what might be? Love bears all things, hopes all things, believes all things, endures all things (1 Corinthians 13:7). . . .

The woman weeping with her husband has a vision. This requires more of her than what she is hoping for in him. She has a hope that her husband might not flee in the midst of her sadness, that he would be present with her, a strong companion. As she offers tears without demanding he respond perfectly, she wears hope's garments—tenderness, strength, and honor. Waiting in hope is never without honor.

## think

- What do you hope for that you don't have?
- Why do you need courage to hope for this and to keep hoping?
- Does hope seem foolish to you? Explain.
- Sometimes it's painful to keep hoping. What should we do about that?

## pray

Lord, I hope for . . .

## read twelve lonely years

Luke 8:43-48

In the crowd that day there was a woman who for twelve years had been afflicted with hemorrhages. She had spent every penny she had on doctors but not one had been able to help her. She slipped in from behind and touched the edge of Jesus' robe. At that very moment her hemorrhaging stopped. Jesus said, "Who touched me?"

When no one stepped forward, Peter said, "But Master, we've got crowds of people on our hands. Dozens have touched you."

Jesus insisted, "Someone touched me. I felt power discharging from me."

When the woman realized that she couldn't remain hidden, she knelt trembling before him. In front of all the people, she blurted out her story—why she touched him and how at that same moment she was healed.

Jesus said, "Daughter, you took a risk trusting me, and now you're healed and whole. Live well, live blessed!"

## think

- Bleeding made this woman ritually unclean, so people would have avoided touching her. Describe the disappointments she may have endured for twelve years.
- What does it take to hope after so many years of disappointment?
- How is your story like this woman's story? How is it different?

# think (continued)

# pray

Master, the risk of trusting you is . . .

## read i'm asking for one thing

Psalm 27

Light, space, zest—
    that's God!
So, with him on my side I'm fearless,
    afraid of no one and nothing.

When vandal hordes ride down
    ready to eat me alive,
Those bullies and toughs
    fall flat on their faces.

When besieged,
    I'm calm as a baby.
When all hell breaks loose,
    I'm collected and cool.

I'm asking God for one thing,
    only one thing:
To live with him in his house
    my whole life long.
I'll contemplate his beauty;
    I'll study at his feet.

That's the only quiet, secure place
    in a noisy world,
The perfect getaway,
    far from the buzz of traffic.
God holds me head and shoulders
    above all who try to pull me down.
I'm headed for his place to offer anthems
    that will raise the roof!
Already I'm singing God-songs;
    I'm making music to God.

Listen, GOD, I'm calling at the top of my lungs:
    "Be good to me! Answer me!"
When my heart whispered, "Seek God,"
    my whole being replied,
"I'm seeking him!"
    Don't hide from me now!

You've always been right there for me;
    Don't turn your back on me now.
Don't throw me out, don't abandon me;
    You've always kept the door open.
My father and mother walked out and left me,
    but GOD took me in.

Point me down your highway, GOD;
    direct me along a well-lighted street;
    show my enemies whose side you're on.
Don't throw me to the dogs,
    those liars who are out to get me,
    filling the air with their threats.

I'm sure now I'll see God's goodness
    in the exuberant earth.
Stay with GOD!
    Take heart. Don't quit.
I'll say it again:
    Stay with GOD.

## think

- What does the writer of this psalm hope and long for?
- How do those hopes compare to what you hope and long for?
- Does truly seeking God mean not wanting things like a husband, children, friends, and career very much? Explain.

- What help for dealing with disappointment does this psalm offer?

## pray

Listen, GOD, I'm calling at the top of my lungs . . .

# read   the sweet by-and-by

Isaiah 25:6-8

> Here on this mountain, GOD-of-the-Angel-Armies
>     will throw a feast for all the people of the world,
> A feast of the finest foods, a feast with vintage wines,
>     a feast of seven courses, a feast lavish with gourmet desserts.
> And here on this mountain, GOD will banish
>     the pall of doom hanging over all peoples,
> The shadow of doom darkening all nations.
>     Yes, he'll banish death forever.
> And GOD will wipe the tears from every face.
>     He'll remove every sign of disgrace
> From his people, wherever they are.
>     Yes! GOD says so!

Revelation 21:1-5

> I saw Heaven and earth new-created. Gone the first Heaven, gone the first earth, gone the sea.
>
> I saw Holy Jerusalem, new-created, descending resplendent out of Heaven, as ready for God as a bride for her husband.
>
> I heard a voice thunder from the Throne: "Look! Look! God has moved into the neighborhood, making his home with men and women! They're his people, he's their God. He'll wipe every tear from their eyes. Death is gone for good—tears gone, crying gone, pain gone—all the first order of things gone." The Enthroned continued, "Look! I'm making everything new."

## think

- Imagine your ultimate future (heaven, resurrection) as a feast. What foods will be served there? Whom would you like to sit and talk with there?

- Imagine your life beyond death, tears, and pain. What do you feel when you think about that?
- Does hoping for this future make you more willing to engage with people and risk disappointment now? Or does it make you want to disengage and coast until then? Why is that?
- If the hope of heaven doesn't do much for you, what about it doesn't inspire you?

## pray

Lord, the hope of heaven makes me . . .

# LIVE

This is the end of *Waking Up from the Dream of a Lifetime*, but it's not the end of the story for you. Hopefully you've discovered some truths about yourself and your disappointments. Take some time now to pull the threads together and make a plan for moving forward. Depending on your situation, your plan may involve taking action in a situation where you've been too passive, or yielding control to God in an area where you've been reluctant to trust him. Do you need to grieve more, or whine less? Get moving, or stop rushing around so frantically? These are the kinds of questions to pray about as you plan your next steps.

- What thoughts about hope do you definitely want to discuss with your small group?

- You probably can't give equal attention to all of the issues raised in this study. What are the key things God has been trying to say to you about one or more of the following?

Disappointment

Your marriage or singleness

Work

Your children or lack of children

Church or other community of believers

Relationship with God

Resilience

- How have your practical steps in these areas been going?

- How will God's truth influence what you do in the next week, next month, and next year?

- How can your small group help you get there?

# notes

lesson 1

1. Jan Meyers, *The Allure of Hope: God's Pursuit of a Woman's Heart* (Colorado Springs, Colo.: NavPress, 2001), pp. 15, 18.
2. Dr. Joyce Brothers, "Quiz: Do You Feel Too Sorry for Yourself?" *Good Housekeeping*, January 2003, Vol. 236, Issue 1.

lesson 2

1. Jeanne Braselton, *A False Sense of Well Being* (New York: Random House, 2001), pp. 12-13.
2. Carrie Gerlach, *Emily's Reasons Why Not* (New York: William Morrow, 2004), pp. 1-2.
3. Virginia McInerney, "The Toughest Questions Singles Ask," *Today's Christian Woman*, May/June 2004.
4. David P. Gushee, "When Marriage Brings Suffering," *Books and Culture*, September/October 2004, pp. 22-23, 40.
5. Mike Mason, *The Mystery of Marriage: Meditations on the Miracle* (Portland, Ore.: Multnomah, 1985), p. 172.

lesson 3

1. Carol Kent, *Secret Longings of the Heart: Overcoming Deep Disappointment and Unfulfilled Expectations* (Colorado Springs, Colo.: NavPress, 2003), p. 149-150.
2. Mihaly Csikszentmihalyi, *Finding Flow: The Psychology of Engagement with Everyday Life* (New York: Basic Books, 1997), pp. 2-3.

lesson 4

1. Lynn Harris, "I'm Disappointed in My Daughter," *Ladies' Home Journal*, July 1994, Vol. 111, Issue 7.
2. Kevin Huggins, *Parenting Adolescents* (Colorado Springs, Colo.: NavPress, 1989), pp. 150-151.

3. Judith Newman, "You Can Get Over Disappointment," *Good Housekeeping*, January 2003, Vol. 236, Issue 1.

lesson 5

1. Research by the Barna Research Group, quoted in Tim Stafford, "The Church—Why Bother?" *Christianity Today*, January 2005, p. 42. "Don't go to church" is defined as "have not been to church in the last six months, apart from Christmas or Easter."
2. John Koessler, "Why I Return to the Pews," *Christianity Today*, December 2004, p. 55.
3. Tim Stafford, "The Church—Why Bother?" *Christianity Today*, January 2005, pp. 48-49.
4. Dallas Willard, *Renovation of the Heart: Putting On the Character of Christ* (Colorado Springs, Colo.: NavPress, 2002), pp. 235-236, 238.
5. Leith Anderson, quoted in R. Daniel Reeves and Thomas Tumblin, "Council on Ecclesiology: Preparation and Summaries," for Councils II and III, at Beeson Divinity School (Birmingham, Alabama) and Westminster Theological Seminary (Escondito, California). Unpublished notes.

lesson 6

1. Brennan Manning, "Shipwrecked at the Stable," in C. S. Lewis, et al., *Watch for the Light: Readings for Advent and Christmas* (Maryknoll, N.Y.: Orbis, 2004), http://www.bruderhof.com/articles/Shipwrecked.htm.
2. Carol Kent, *Secret Longings of the Heart: Overcoming Deep Disappointment and Unfulfilled Expectations* (Colorado Springs, Colo.: NavPress, 2003), pp. 71-72.

lesson 7

1. This quiz was created by Al Siebert, Ph.D., author of *The Survivor Personality: Why Some People Are Stronger, Smarter, and More Skillful at Handling Life's Difficulties . . . and How You Can Be, Too.* It appeared in Rubin Stevens and Bonnie Miller, "Secrets of Resilient Women," *Good Housekeeping,* January 2000, Vol. 230, Issue 1, p. 108.
2. Debra Kent, "Six Ways to Deal with Disappointment," *Redbook,* April 1997, Vol. 188, Issue 6.

lesson 8

1. Jan Meyers and Karen Lee-Thorp, *Hope and Joy Will Find You* (Colorado Springs, Colo.: NavPress, 2003), p. 89.
2. Jan Meyers, *The Allure of Hope: God's Pursuit of a Woman's Heart* (Colorado Springs, Colo.: NavPress, 2001), pp. 66-68.

# More life-shaping titles in the
## REAL LIFE STUFF FOR WOMEN *series.*

### Running Nowhere in Every Direction

*On Stress*
1-57683-836-6

Women especially seem to be running as fast as they can—to work, school, church, sports, music lessons, and the mall. Join with other women to discover God's ways to get off the treadmill.

### Peeking into a Box of Chocolates

*On Temptation*
1-57683-835-8

All sorts of temptations allure us every day. This refreshing new discussion guide helps you uncover the core issues behind the temptations and then deal with them one by one in God's forgiving grace.

### Searching for God in a Bottomless Purse

*On Faith*
1-57683-863-3

Filled with stimulating insights and realistic hope, this new Bible study will help you examine the truth of your faith life and build a stronger relationship with God.

Richard Card    bleeding / cancer